The Barefoot Book of Children

written by

Tessa Strickland and Kate DePalma

illustrated by

David Dean

Barefoot Books
Step inside a story

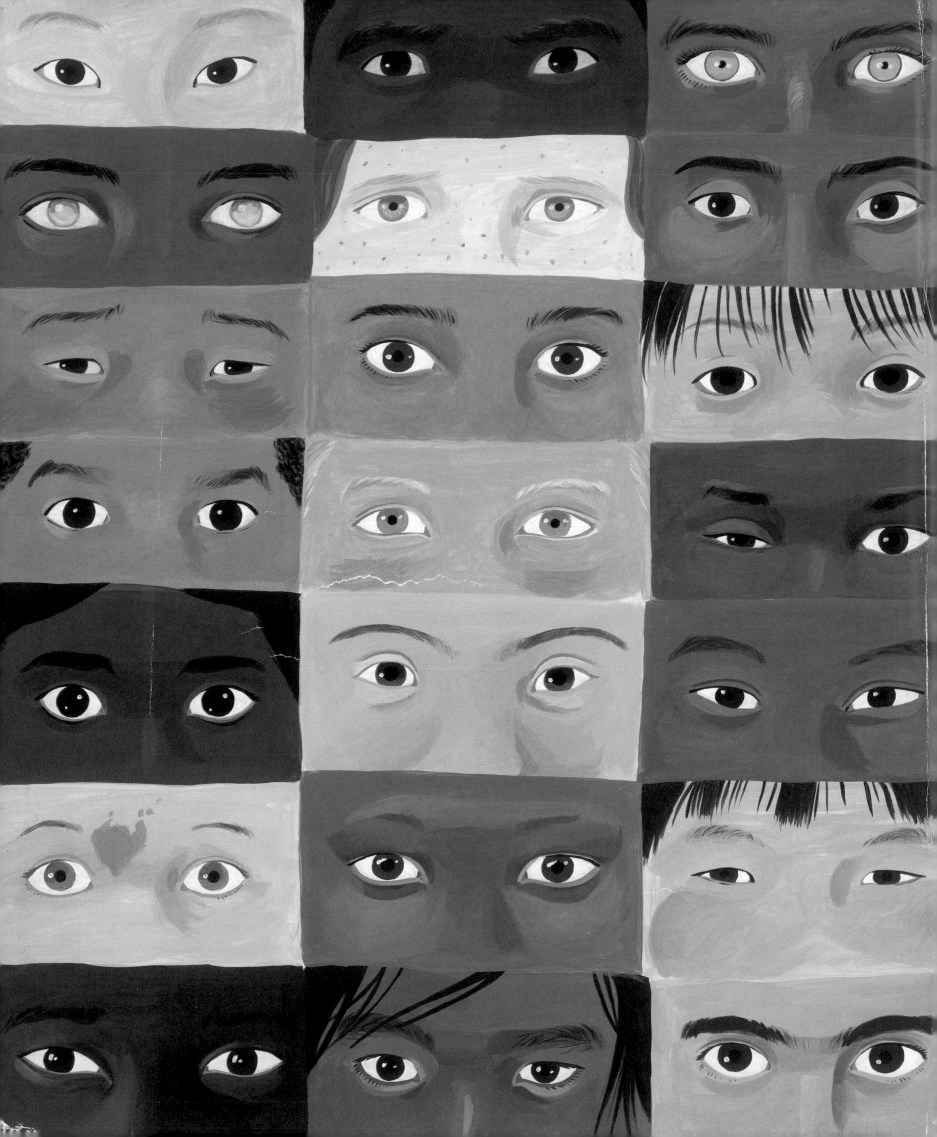

Every morning, millions of children open their eyes
and start another day.

We are all somewhere. Where are you?

What can you see or hear or smell from where you are?

Wherever you are, you need
a place to live. A home can be
just one room, or be so big that
you can get lost inside.

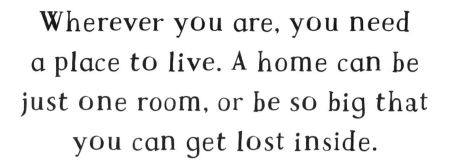

Do you have a special place?
Perhaps a place where you go
when you want to play with
a friend or daydream or just
be quiet for a while?

We all need other people.
People teach us the names of trees,
mend us when we're hurt and rise early
in the morning to bake our bread.

Most children live in families. Your family might be big or small.

Perhaps you have one parent, perhaps you have two.

Some members of your family might live close by.

You might be the only child in your family.
You might have lots of brothers, sisters or cousins.

Maybe you have foster parents or a stepfamily.

Maybe someone you love is far away.

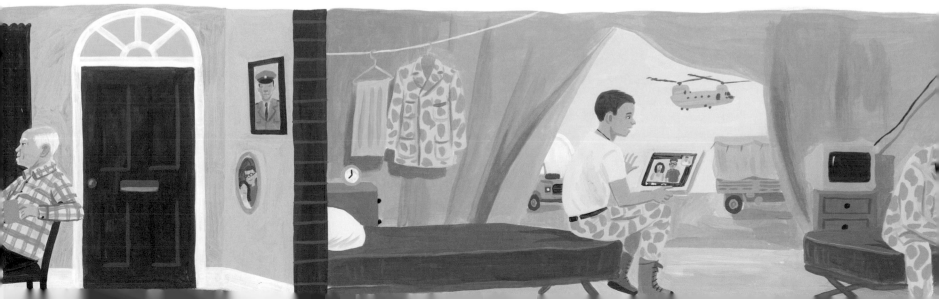

We come in all different shapes and sizes
and hues, like jewels or flowers or fish.
Long legs, small hands, curly hair,
freckled skin, hazel eyes — no two people
have bodies that are just the same.

What you wear can depend on where you live and how you spend your time. Some clothes are for sleeping or playing or for special occasions.

Just putting on a new hat

can make you feel like a different person.

We can all do amazing things.
What do you like to do?
What would you like to do if
you had the chance?

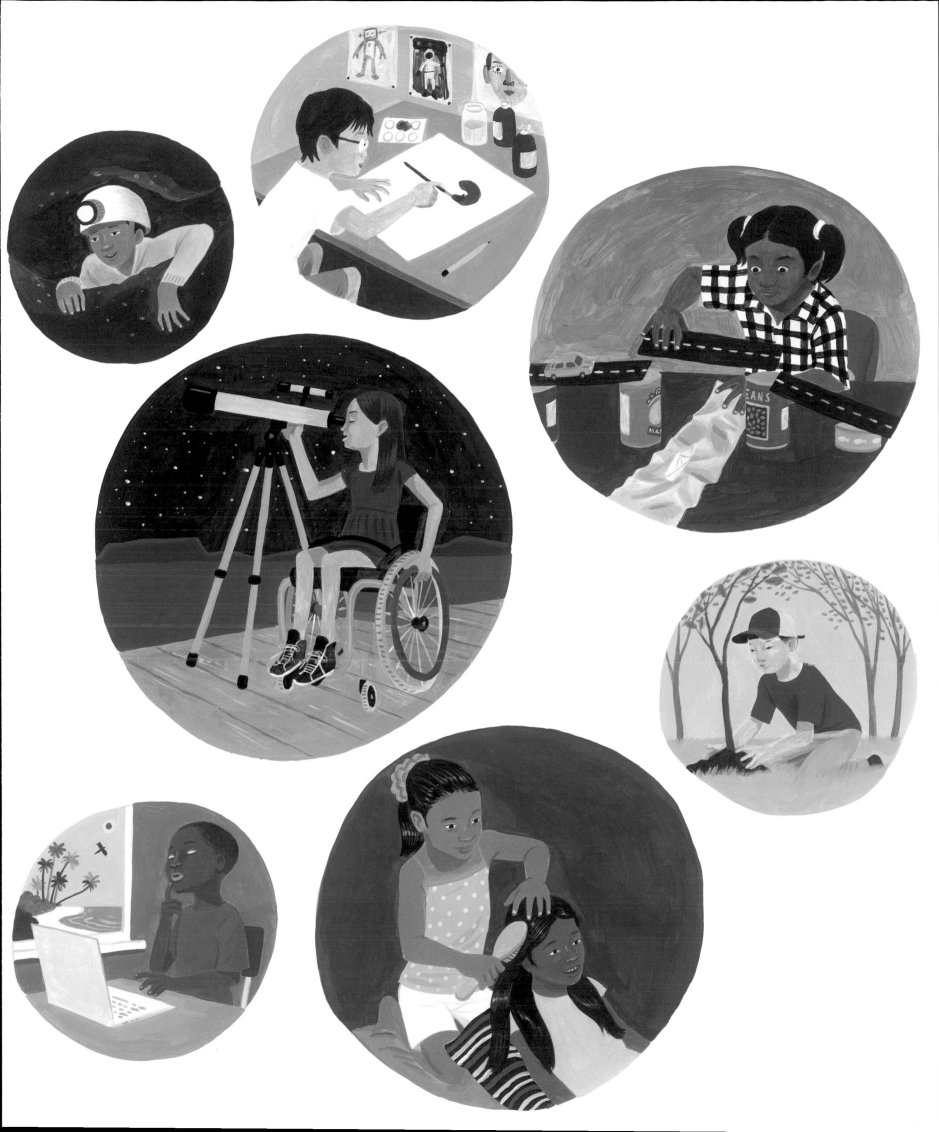

Life is sometimes about play.

Games can be complicated like chess, or simple like hide-and-seek.

Playing is how we learn.

You can play with friends, or you can play alone.

Life is
sometimes
about work too.
Maybe you help
clean up after dinner
or take care of your
baby sister or water the
garden. Maybe you do
jobs to earn pocket
money or help
your family.

We need good food to eat and clean water to drink. At a table, on a rug, with your fingers, with a piece of bread — there are lots of different ways to enjoy a meal. What tastes good to you might taste strange to someone else.

We
need
water
to clean
ourselves
too.

We all have a name.
What's yours?

Does it have
a meaning?

أميرة

Lucia

Lovelie

Maybe you're the only person
who's ever had that name,

Marika

Stefano

Yasmin

اديوش

Konrad

INESE

승기

oydisho

Sisipho

ﾊﾆﾙ

লিরি

or maybe you share your name
with many other people.

РУСЛАН

Do you have a nickname,
like Nanou or Noodle or Red?

Feelings can come and go like weather.
Everyone feels curious or silly
or scared sometimes.

A life is made up of days.
Every day is different,
but some are more special
than others.

Do you sometimes find a way
to make a day or moment
more special — for you or
for someone else?

Do you
have a treasure
that is special to you?
A feather you found on the
beach, or a photo, or a pebble
your granddad gave you
when you were small?
Where do you
keep it?

Some people worship. Some people pray.
Some meditate. Some like quiet time to think.
Some people prefer to take life as it comes.

We all have love to give.
There are lots of ways to show people you care,
like saying sweet things, offering your help
or just spending time with them.

How do you share your love?

Every life is a story.

It's easier to understand someone when you know their story.

You are a part of the world.
You are also a world all your own.
This is where you belong.

What will happen in your story?

A Closer Look at the Illustrations

Are you curious to learn more about the children in this book? Each child is just like you, full of hopes and fears, with talents to share and stories to tell. Whether you want to know more about the children you have met, the types of houses you have seen, the games being played or the languages being spoken, the following pages will give you information about all these things and much more.

But remember, this book only gives you a tiny snapshot of how children live around the world. These scenes show some possibilities, but not the only way people do things in a country or culture. Seeing a child flying a kite in Afghanistan in these pages doesn't mean that's all kids do there, or that children in other places don't enjoy flying kites too. There's a huge world beyond the pages of this book.

Where Are You?

The planet we live on is wonderful and varied. You may live in a city full of the sounds of bustling markets, cars and people, or you may be surrounded by nature where the birds are singing and the wind is rustling the leaves in the trees. You may smell the salt of the ocean or feel the warmth of the sun on your back. Do you know why you live where you live? Perhaps your family has lived there for generations, or perhaps it was a need for safety that brought you. Maybe you moved because someone was offered a job, or to be closer to friends or family. Have you ever lived anywhere else?

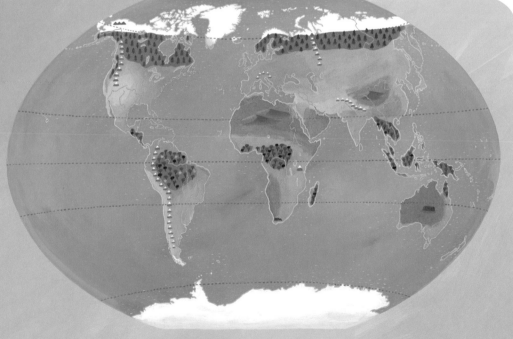

Where on earth are you right now?
Take a look at the map and see if you can find your current location.

Mexico

Suriname

Algeria

Nepal

Czech Republic

Australia

Homes

Wherever you are, you need a place to live. A home can be just one room, or be so big that you can get lost inside.

Have you ever wondered why there are so many different kinds of homes? There are lots of things that influence how homes are made: the climate, the amount of land that's available, the local materials, the number of people who need housing and their way of life. Some people live in the same place all their lives, while others are constantly relocating. At times, children or families may find themselves without a home to live in.

Which one of the homes in this picture would you like to spend the night in? What do you think it would be like?

1. ger (Mongolia)
Gers (or yurts) work well for nomadic people who move three or four times per year because they are quick to put up and resistant to the wind.

3. apartment (United States)
Apartments (or flats), like this one in San Francisco, are homes that take up part of a larger building made up of apartments.

2. farmhouse (Scotland)
Built from stone and normally two floors, Scottish farmhouses were designed to resist wet and windy weather and encourage family, visitors and even furry friends to linger in the warm kitchen.

4. stilt house (Malaysia)
Due to the tropical climate of Malaysia, stilts are important for keeping these wooden houses cool and dry in the warm, wet weather.

5. apartment (Brazil)
In heavily populated cities like Rio de Janeiro, high-rise apartments are an efficient way of housing lots of people in a small land area.

Special Places

Many people have a special place where they like to spend time. These might be quiet places where we can be closer to our own thoughts and feelings or spend time with a friend. A special place can even be imaginary — a place to visit in your mind. Where is your special place? What do you like to do there? How does it make you feel to be there?

China

Morocco

Israel

New Zealand

Italy

People

We look to other people to meet our basic human needs, like having food in our bellies, clothes on our backs and a home to live in. Whether we're eating *mischbrot* (sourdough rye bread) in Germany or *injera* (spongy flatbread) in Ethiopia, we all depend on other people to help us every day.

We also need people who care for us, like doctors and nurses. These people help us when we're sick or hurt, and can also help us stay healthy — for example, children all over the world get shots called vaccines to try to prevent illnesses.

And as we grow up, we need others to help us learn about the world. Teachers can impact our lives whether or not we get a chance to go to school. From the dense woodlands of Finland to the lush rain forests of Bolivia, children look to family, friends and educators to teach them about the world.

Can you think of all the people who help you in different ways?

Germany   **Ethiopia**   **South Africa**   **Pakistan**

Finland   **Bolivia**

Families

Who do you think of when you hear the word *family*? You may immediately think of a grandparent or another relative, or you may think of a close friend who never misses a family picnic.

Some families are created by a birth, and some families are created through adoption. Some children find a home with foster parents — people who care for them and give them a safe place to live and grow.

Some children have a mother or a father, some have two mothers or two fathers, and some have a mother and a father. But these are just a few of the ways a family can look. Families can also change over time — perhaps growing with the addition of a new baby or a stepfamily member.

There are so many different kinds of families. Can you name some of the people in your family?

Bodies

Of everyone who has ever lived, no two people have ever had bodies that are just the same — even identical twins. People come in different shapes, sizes and skin tones, and every face is unique. Different bodies can have different abilities, and you will meet people in your life whose bodies work differently than yours — maybe because their bodies have always been a certain way, or maybe because their bodies have changed. Every body changes over the course of a life. But no matter what a person's body looks like, it doesn't change who they are on the inside. People who look very different can be friends, or might even be part of the same family.

Some people feel comfortable in the bodies they were born in, but others might like their bodies to be different. Think about your own body and how clever, complex and multi-skilled it is. There's no body quite like your body!

Hats

People wear hats for many reasons — to protect their heads, to celebrate an occasion or just to show their personal style. Does wearing a hat make you feel special?

Clothes

People have different clothes for different occasions. If we're heading to bed, we want to wear something comfortable for sleeping. If we're going to take part in sports, we need to have footwear that supports us well and clothing that doesn't restrict our movement. Often sports teams will have a uniform, which helps members to feel a sense of belonging. In fact, there are lots of types of uniform — for school, clubs and hobbies. Have you ever worn one?

Our clothes also need to suit the weather where we live. A snowsuit will keep you warm even on the coldest of winter days, but in hot, sunny weather, light, cool clothes are probably more comfortable. We may have heaps of clothes or wear the same ones every day. Clothes can be a way of expressing who we are and what we like to do. Do you have an outfit you like best? How do you feel when you wear it?

Hobbies

Hobbies are our interests. We might share a hobby with a group of friends or family, or we might have one of our own. Hobbies can be about trying new experiences, like exploring caves or learning nautical skills in the Sea Cadet Corps. Hobbies can be also about making things, like creating gravity-powered cars to race or building dens out of natural materials to play in. No matter what you like to do, putting time into your chosen hobby can help you gain confidence and skill. What are your hobbies?

diving
(Portugal)

illustration
(Japan)

engineering
(Mauritius)

robotics
(Iran)

building gravity racers
(Kenya)

caving
(Saudi Arabia)

building dens
(England)

ballet dancing
(Russia)

astronomy
(Australia)

planting trees
(South Korea)

hairdressing
(Nicaragua)

Sea Cadet Corps
(Wales)

writing
(Angola)

Play

We tend to play because it is fun, but we learn a lot while we do it — how to communicate with others, how to win and lose well, and all about the world around us. Playing can simply mean using your imagination — who would you like to pretend to be today?

1. kites (Afghanistan)
In windy Afghanistan, flying kites is not just a hobby — it is an art form! In the sport of kite fighting, competitors try to cut other fliers' kites down by slicing through their strings.

2. cat's cradle (Thailand)
Cat's cradle is a game in which fingers are used to make shapes with a piece of string that's passed between two players. Children have taught one another to play for generations.

3. ice hockey (Canada)
Ice hockey was first developed in Canada over 100 years ago, and it is considered the official winter sport of Canada. It is mainly played in countries with cold winters, but with indoor ice rinks it can be played anywhere all year round.

4. rock-paper-scissors (China)
Rock-paper-scissors is a simple game for two people. On the count of three, each player makes one of their hands into a shape. Rock breaks scissors, scissors cut paper, and paper covers rock. The game probably originated in China before becoming popular in Japan (where it is called *jan-ken*) and beyond.

5. chess (Russia)
Chess has been played for thousands of years, making it one of the oldest games in the world. To win you must defeat your opponent's army of pieces and capture their king.

6. hide-and-seek (United States)
Hide-and-seek can be played by children of almost any age, who speak any language, in just about any location. One person closes their eyes and counts while the others scatter to hiding places. Have you ever played?

7. skipping rope (Jamaica)
Cooperation, rhythm, singing and exercise are just some of the benefits of playing with a skipping rope or jump rope. With a long rope, several children can skip together, making this a popular playground game.

8. cricket (India)
Cricket started as a game with sticks and a ball in England several hundred years ago, and is now played in countries as widespread as Australia, India and Jamaica. Two teams of eleven players take turns to bowl and bat, trying to score the most runs (points).

9. kendama (Japan)
Kendama is an individual challenge using a special wooden stick with a ball attached by string. The skill lies in being able to catch the ball in one of the two cups on either side of the stick or on the point at the end. It's very tricky!

10. puzzle (France)
Jigsaws were originally pictures painted on wood, then cut up into small pieces using a tool known as a jigsaw. Now they are commonly made of cardboard but the goal is the same — to put the picture back together again by fitting the pieces together.

Work

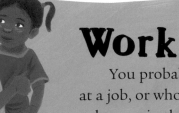

You probably know a lot of adults who go to work at a job, or whose work is to take care of the family or volunteer in the community. Just like grown-ups, kids can help their families and communities by doing different types of work. Work can challenge us and teach us new skills. It's satisfying to know that we've done our work as well as we can.

Your work might include helping with jobs at home, looking after siblings, doing school homework or working outside the home to earn an income. Although a lot of work is paid, many aspects of life also rely on people giving their time for free. What do you do to help your family? What do they do to help you?

babysitting
(Bangladesh)

herding cattle
(Tanzania)

herding reindeer
(Norway)

washing dishes (Thailand)

hanging out laundry (Australia)

harvesting grapes
(Chile)

grooming dog
(Canada)

Baths

Many people take their baths and showers indoors, but a plunge in a nearby lake is another effective way of getting clean. While many of us bathe alone or with siblings at home, a trip to the hot springs in countries like Japan to bathe with others can be a sociable experience or even a tourist attraction.

Bathing plays an important role in keeping us healthy and avoiding infections. It plays other roles too: perhaps waking us up in the morning or relaxing us in the evening. How do you like to bathe? Do you sing while you scrub?

Hungary

Vietnam

Ireland

Ghana

New Zealand

Japan

Food

The food we eat depends on what grows nearby, what our local shops and markets sell and what we can afford. Our diet varies through the seasons and can be influenced by our beliefs, culture and even allergies. Although many foods are associated with a certain culture, people enjoy all different kinds of food all over the world. You can eat sushi in Italy or pizza in Japan. What do you like to eat?

diri ak pwa (Haiti)

Containing the classic Caribbean ingredients of rice and beans, *diri ak pwa* is a highly nutritious meal. The beans are often homegrown and can be pinto, kidney or black beans.

pizza (Italy)

The origins of pizza actually go as far back as the Greeks and Romans, but it was the Italians who added the tomato and cheese that we enjoy today.

shepherd's pie (England)

A very traditional meal, shepherd's pie (or cottage pie if made with beef rather than lamb) has a meat base with onions, carrots and peas, with mashed potatoes on top.

dal makhani (India)

The name of this dish means "buttery lentil." It is a thick stew often prepared in the Punjab region of India and Pakistan that is made of black lentils with red kidney beans, butter and cream.

juriltai shul (Mongolia)

Mongolian dishes are influenced by Mongolia's cold climate and its contact with China and Russia. *Juriltai shul* brings together meat, noodles and vegetables to create a hearty soup.

chicken satay (Indonesia)

This popular dish of seasoned meat grilled on a skewer is sold at roadside stalls and fancy restaurants alike. It is usually served with peanut sauce.

borscht (Ukraine)

Eaten cold in summer and hot in winter, borscht gets its incredible red appearance from beetroots, which are the main ingredient of this sweet and sour soup.

peri-peri prawns (Mozambique)

Mozambique's extensive coastline means that seafood is widely eaten and very fresh. Peri-peri prawns are spiced up with paprika, peppers, garlic and lemon to tickle the taste buds.

clam chowder (United States)

New England boasts the most famous of all clam chowders — a thick, creamy soup packed full of clams, potatoes and onions, then served with a sprinkling of crackers on top.

ajiaco (Colombia)

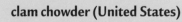

Chicken, corn and three different types of potato make up this comforting soup. Known for their creamy texture, *papa criolla* potatoes are very popular in Colombia.

cuy chactado (Peru)

People in Peru have been eating *cuy* or guinea pig for about 5,000 years. They are flattened under stones, fried and then eaten by hand. Also popular is *olluquito con charqui*, a dish made from root vegetables and alpaca.

miso udon soup (Japan)

Miso, a fermented soybean paste, provides a key taste in many Japanese foods. Udon are thick, white noodles popular in soups and eaten by scooping them up with chopsticks. Also well-known are many types of sushi, often made of raw fish, rice and seaweed.

pickled herring (Sweden)

Usually served with potatoes, hard-boiled eggs, sour cream and a type of crispbread known as *knäckebröd*, herring have been eaten as a pickled delicacy in Sweden since the Middle Ages. What type would you choose: garlic and dill, onion or mustard?

thiéboudienne (Senegal)

The main ingredients of *thiéboudienne* are fish, rice and tomato sauce with a mild blend of spices. Usually served in a large communal dish, it is eaten by hand. In other countries it is also known as *riz graz* or Jollof rice.

hummus (Syria)

Made from roasted chickpeas, hummus has become incredibly popular far beyond its original home in the eastern Mediterranean. Pita (or pitta) bread is great for scooping up the creamy hummus, which is often eaten with tabbouleh, a salad made of cracked wheat, tomatoes, parsley and mint.

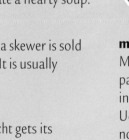

Languages

Everyone finds a way to communicate somehow — often through speech but also by gesture or body language. There are thousands of languages spoken and written worldwide, with different styles of script and alphabets as well as varying dialects and pronunciation.

1. Thai
ขอกินก๋วยเตี๋ยวนะครับแม่
ได้จ้ะลูก ไป ไปกินกัน
  Can I have some noodles, Mom?
  Yes, son. Let's go eat.

2. Polish
Uważaj!
Przepraszam — nie widziałem cię!
  Look out!
  Sorry — I didn't see you!

3. Greek
Τι ὤρα φεύγει το επόμενο τρένο για Φιλαντέλφια;
Σε δέκα λεπτά από την πλατφόρμα 6.
  When's the next train to Philadelphia?
  It leaves from Platform 6 in 10 minutes.

4. Spanish
¡Ay no, nos cancelaron el tren!
Vamos a comer algo en lo que llega otro.
  Oh no! Our train's been cancelled!
  Let's go get something to eat while we wait for another one.

5. English
Excuse me, do you know where the taxis are?
Yes — go out the exit over there.

6. Yoruba
Sé gbogbo wa lati wà níbí?
Mi ò rí Folá.
Òun nì yen, níbi èro tíkétì.
  Are we all here?
  I don't see Folá.
  There she is, at the ticket line.

7. Arabic
لقد فقدت تذكرتي
إلق نظرة أخرى في كل جيوبك
  I lost my ticket.
  Take another look in all your pockets.

8. Hebrew
כמה זמן תארך הנסיעה?
היא אמורה לקחת ארבע שעות.
  How long is the journey?
  It should take 4 hours.

9. Mandarin
我们需要找询问柜台。
看，就在那里！
  We need to find the information desk.
  Look, it's over there!

10. Japanese
自撮りしよう！
  Let's take a selfie.

11. Hindi
बाथरूम कहाँ है ?
  Where's the bathroom?

12. Korean
이 기계 어떻게 쓰는지 아세요?
  Do you know how this machine works?

13. Tagalog
Kamusta ang biyahe mo?
  Hi! How was your journey?

14. American Sign Language

  Did you ride the train?

Names

What's your name? Do people use your full name, shorten it or maybe just call you by your initials? Names may be chosen for their meaning, to celebrate a special person or simply because people like the way they look or sound. Your name is a part of you from the moment it is given to you, but your name might change when you get older. What names do you like?

Lucia
"bringer of light"
Portuguese

Lovelie
"beautiful"
Haitian Creole

Stefano
"crown"
Italian

We all have a name. What's yours?

Does it have a meaning?

Maybe you're the only person who's ever had that name.

or maybe you share your name with many other people.

Do you have a nickname, like Nanou or Noodle or Red?

Victor
"winner"
Spanish

Marika
"quiet"
Maori

Darnell
"hidden"
English

داريوش
(or *Darioush*)
"rich and kingly"
Farsi

Konrad
"honest advisor"
German

Inese
"holy"
Latvian

슬기
(or *Seul-gi*)
"wisdom"
Korean

أميرة
(or *Amira*)
"princess"
Arabic

Sisipho
"gift"
Xhosa

አበበ
(or *Abebe*)
"blooming"
Amharic

Руслан
(or *Ruslan*)
"lion"
Russian

শিরীন
(or *Shirin*)
"sweet"
Bengali

Ni Luh
"first-born girl"
Javanese

Feelings

Feelings are the way we respond to the world around us, the people we meet and the experiences we have. Sometimes we feel so joyful that we want to skip, jump, sing or shout. Other times, we can feel so sad and worried that we want to hide away from everything until we feel better. Some situations make us nervous — as if we have butterflies in our belly. Other situations make us feel proud — as if we might burst with happiness. But what makes one person feel happy can leave another feeling scared. It's important to try to be aware of how you feel, talk to people about your emotions and express them in a way that doesn't hurt others. Notice how the people around you are feeling too — maybe you could help them by listening to them or playing with them.

How do you think these children feel?

Special Days

As the years go by, particular days stand out to us as special. This may be due to annual celebrations like birthdays, Hanukkah or Halloween. On these occasions, we take time to make people we care about feel important, perhaps buy presents, eat festive food or dress up. Other days we may remember for more personal reasons — a loved one returning home after a long absence, a new member joining the family or just time spent with someone special. While some of these days may involve private and small celebrations, some festivals may include the entire community, region, country or even the whole world.

Hanukkah
(France)

Halloween
(Puerto Rico)

birthday party
(United States)

mehndi painting
(India)

homecoming
(Netherlands)

Carnival
(Saint Kitts)

new sibling
(Andorra)

playing together
(Singapore)

red envelope (China)
Filled with money by family and friends, children love receiving these envelopes at Chinese New Year. You might call them *lai see*, *ang pao*, *hong bao* or another name depending upon where you live.

nazar (Turkey)
Made from glass with circles that look like an eye, people carry this bead to keep away bad luck.

conker (England)
The game of conkers is played by attaching the seed of a chestnut tree to a piece of string. Two players then battle it out to see which conker is stronger by striking them against each other.

Treasures

Some of us own too many things to count, and others have almost nothing at all. But everyone has something they treasure. We gather treasures because they remind us of feelings and experiences. What's your most special treasure?

arrowheads (United States)
Arrowheads are chipped out of materials like stone to make them sharp, then attached to a stick to form an arrow that can be shot by a bow.

note (Iceland)
This note says "Have a great day, honey. Hugs and kisses. — Mama" in Icelandic. Have you kept notes or letters from anyone?

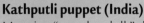
Eigðu góðan dag elskan.
knús og kossar.
- Mamma

bracelet (Burkina Faso)
Bracelets like this one from Burkina Faso are made from recycled materials by people all over the world.

Kathputli puppet (India)
Meaning "wooden doll," these string puppets have been created for Indian children for over a thousand years and remain popular today.

Faith

Some people worship. Some people pray.
Some meditate. Some like quiet time to think.
Some people prefer to take life as it comes.

Faith has many meanings — some people believe in one deity, some people believe in many deities and some don't believe in any deity at all. Some people aren't sure what they believe. We display our faith in different ways — regular visits to religious buildings, particular rituals or celebrations on special dates. Beliefs can be very personal and important. No matter what we believe in, learning about other people's beliefs can help us understand them better.

1. singing (Eastern Orthodoxy)
Music is important in many faiths. Eastern Orthodox services are conducted almost entirely in song.

2. congregation (Judaism)
Sometimes people gather together to worship on a holiday or on a certain day of the week. Jewish people might go to synagogue for services on Shabbat, the day of rest.

3. Bharatanatyam dancing (Hinduism)
Some spiritual traditions use dance as part of their sacred rituals, giving physical expression to their beliefs.

4. Holy Communion (Roman Catholicism)
Holy Communion reminds Catholics of the Last Supper, when Jesus shared bread and wine with his apostles, with the bread as his body and the wine as his blood.

5. meditation
Meditation is a simple and effective way of quieting the body and exploring the nature of the mind. People of many different faiths meditate, as well as people who don't follow a faith tradition.

6. Shichi-Go-San ceremony (Shintoism)
This ceremony, which means "seven-five-three," celebrates the health and well being of young children. It includes a visit to a local Shinto shrine.

7. visiting a mosque (Islam)
When Muslims, who follow the religion of Islam, visit a mosque to worship, they remove their shoes and wash before they pray.

8. collecting alms (Buddhism)
In some Buddhist countries, boys join monasteries for a short period of time as part of their education. During this time, they collect alms or gifts every day, depending on food that is donated by others to feed themselves.

9. children in nature
Many people feel a sense of wonder when they are surrounded by the beauty of nature.

Love

A letter, a hug, a squeeze or a kiss — all are ways that we share and show our love. Invisible but everywhere — can you feel the love around you?

United States (Mississippi)   **United States (Colorado)**

Hong Kong

Papua New Guinea

Panama

Sri Lanka

Belgium

Serbia

Stories

There are millions of children on earth, each one leading a life all their own — just like you do! Think about how many places you go, people you meet and activities you enjoy just in a single day. But no matter how many adventures you have in your life, there will always be more things you can learn about the world and about other people.

Learning about others allows us to experience a richer life than we could if we never looked beyond our own experiences. Books are one way we can learn about other people's stories. Would you like to hear more about some of the children you have met in this book? Can you find where you have seen these four children before?

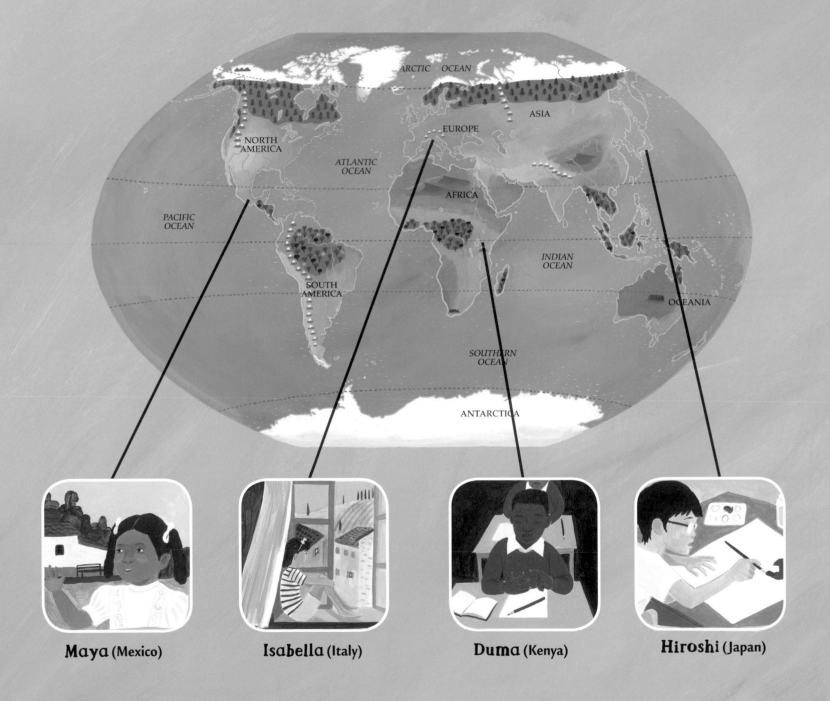

Maya (Mexico)   **Isabella** (Italy)   **Duma** (Kenya)   **Hiroshi** (Japan)

Take a moment to think about your life. What are some of your most special memories? Can you think of a time when you learned something important? What do you still want to try?

As we grow, we become more able to shape who we are, what we want from our lives and our future. What kind of person will you be?

Duma (Kenya)

Shall we find out what Duma has been up to? Every morning begins with a hearty breakfast in his bungalow on the outskirts of Nairobi. He lives there with his sister, Mahiri, and his parents. Duma and Mahiri head off to school on the bus. He tries to concentrate but can't wait to get home and work on his go-cart. Duma manages to put the final wheel on before it's time for a haircut. Which part of his day looks most fun to you?

Isabella (Italy)

Meet Isabella, our friend in San Gimignano, Tuscany. She lives with her father and her cat, Salvatore, in a little old house in the middle of town. When she's not playing the piano or reading with her father, she likes to watch the world go by her window. Isabella prefers to be inside much of the time. Sometimes large crowds and big spaces seem overwhelming to her.

The Easter celebrations are approaching, so Isabella has been busy painting eggs, which will soon decorate their house. Just before she climbs into bed each night, she likes to say her prayers. What do you do before you get into bed?

Hiroshi (Japan)

It looks like Hiroshi is having an exciting day in Osaka. After he has been to the shops to buy food, he finds time for the hobby he likes best: painting. There is no school for him today as it's Children's Day, held each year on May 5. The banners are shaped like carp, a type of fish, which represent each member of the family and look like they are swimming as they flutter in the breeze. Because it's a holiday, Hiroshi has time to play with his sister and friends before they all sit down for a family meal. What do you do when you have a day off from school?

Maya (Mexico)

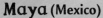

Maya is enjoying a celebration known as the Day of the Dead. She lives in San Lorenzo Texmelucan, a small village in rural Oaxaca, a state in southern Mexico. She needs to make sure she hangs out the washing where the goats won't come and pull it down! She loves to help her mother, choosing the food for dinner and making a special type of bread, known as *pan de muerto* or bread of the dead. In the evening, they visit the graves of their departed family to light candles and leave offerings. It's a fun and festive occasion. The candles look beautiful, don't they?

The Cover

No matter where we live or how we live, we are all connected. Take a close look at the front and back covers of this book. The details in the artwork represent the interconnectedness of our world. What connections can you find?

 How many mangoes can you count?

Find the child writing a postcard. Can you see where he sent it?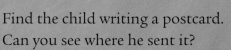

 Would you rather have Nigerian seafood *banga* soup or Filipino *arroz valenciana* for dinner tonight?

Find the child playing with blocks. Can you find the shape she's making somewhere else on the cover?

 Would you rather try painting Easter eggs in Lithuania or playing tag with monks in Burma?

Find the child painting on an easel. Can you find the children he's painting? Can you find another child working at an easel?

 Would you rather try sewing a patchwork *bojagi* cloth in South Korea, or see the famous striped water towers in Kuwait City, Kuwait?

Authors' Note

We wrote *The Barefoot Book of Children* to invite young readers to explore the world and discover their place within it. Creating it has been a joy, and also a huge challenge. It's impossible to make a book about the children of the world that will represent every experience. So we decided to focus on what we have in common. We have learned so much while exploring the customs and ways of life that make the lives of children so varied. But at the core of this book are the values that are shared the world over, wherever our homes happen to be.

At a time when global communication and travel are faster than they have ever been before, *The Barefoot Book of Children* is also an invitation to slow down. We invite you to explore this book again and again, using the ideas in it as a springboard for sharing and discussion. You'll find something new in David Dean's amazing illustrations every time you look at it. One world, many children. One world, many stories. What's yours?

— Tessa Strickland and Kate DePalma

Illustrator's Note

My first step for any project is to learn about the subject. Research is as important for an artist as painting the finished artwork. *The Barefoot Book of Children* touches on many different cultures and ideas and topics, so I had a lot of questions to answer in my research. *What do children eat in Peru? What happens at a ceremony in a Shinto temple? What would you see for sale at a market in Mexico?* I have a collection of books on a wide variety of topics, but these days I do much of my research online. I have saved over 3000 reference images for this book alone!

Cover artwork in progress

Paint palette for Food artwork

I start each morning with a walk through the countryside, which gives me time to plan my day in my head. Then I spend most of the day working in my (usually cluttered!) studio with occasional visits from my two cats. When I'm sketching my ideas, I might use either a sketchbook or a digital tablet. For the final illustrations, I paint on paperboard using heavy-body acrylic paint, which is so thick and smooth that it feels like painting with clotted cream. I prefer quiet when I'm working on research, but when I'm painting, I listen to music.

Working on this book has put me in touch with my inner child. I especially enjoyed creating the Houses page, because I loved complex illustrations like that when I was small. I had so much fun planning the homes and decorating them. I also included some details from my own childhood in this book, like the tatty one-eyed cloth cat on the Treasures page. I took inspiration from many places to create this book, and I hope the experience of reading it will inspire young readers to create something special of their own.

— David Dean

Treasures artwork in progress

Still curious?

You can learn more about the places you've visited in this book in our *Barefoot Books World Atlas* and meet more children from all over the world with other global stories from our Barefoot Books library. There's no telling where you'll go!

Barefoot Books is more than a publisher — we empower passionate people to **share** stories, **connect** families and **inspire** children in their communities and beyond. Visit our website to learn more about how you can join our movement!

Artwork by David Dean from *Barefoot Books World Atlas*

To Francis, Rollo and Zoë, who are forever and always my greatest inspiration — T. S.
For my precious child, Sasha, and for Julia, who was a child with me — K. D.
For Mum and Dad — D. D.

Thank you!

The authors are indebted to many people for their help in the creation of this book, especially:
- Alexandra Strick and Beth Cox, Founders of Inclusive Minds (UK)
- María-Verónica A. Barnes, Director of Diversity Education at Lexington Montessori School (Lexington, MA, USA)
- Stefanie Paige Grossman, M. S. Ed., Child Development Specialist

Barefoot Books, 2067 Massachusetts Ave, Cambridge, MA 02140
Barefoot Books, 29/30 Fitzroy Square, London, W1T 6LQ

Text copyright © 2016 by Tessa Strickland and Kate DePalma
Illustration guide text by Tessa Strickland, Kate DePalma and Emma Parkin
Illustrations copyright © 2016 by David Dean
The moral rights of Tessa Strickland, Kate DePalma and David Dean have been asserted

First published in the United States of America by Barefoot Books, Inc
and in Great Britain by Barefoot Books, Ltd in 2016
All rights reserved

Graphic design by Sarah Soldano, Barefoot Books
Art directed by Tessa Strickland and Kate DePalma, Barefoot Books
Reproduction by Bright Arts, Hong Kong. Printed in Canada on 100% acid-free paper
This book was typeset in Mr. Anteater, ITC Legacy Serif and Legacy Sans ITC Std
The illustrations were prepared in heavy-body acrylics on 400gsm Bristol Board

ISBN 978-1-78285-296-4

Library of Congress Cataloging-in-Publication Data is available upon request

British Cataloguing-in-Publication Data: a catalogue record for this book
is available from the British Library

1 3 5 7 9 8 6 4 2

Tessa Strickland was brought up in rural north England, the second of five children. She spent her childhood amid hens, horses and haystacks, and could often be found immersed in books or exploring the local woods and fields on her pony. A succession of interesting guests from around the world passed through her parents' house, kindling a lasting interest in other cultures. Tessa co-founded Barefoot Books with Nancy Traversy in the early 1990s, and has gone on to create many highly acclaimed children's books, including the numerous books she has written as Stella Blackstone. She is also mother to three adult children, a yoga practitioner and a licensed psychotherapist. Tessa now lives and works in Somerset, southwest England, where she no longer has a pony but makes up for it by owning a handsome black-and-white rocking horse.

Kate DePalma was born and raised outside Nashville, TN, USA. As a child, she enjoyed wholesome activities like making up stories and catching crawdads almost as much as she enjoyed playing pranks and dressing up like Whitney Houston to go with her mom to the grocery store. As Senior Editor at Barefoot Books, she has helped develop dozens of picture books, including *My Big Barefoot Book of Wonderful Words*, which she wrote and art directed with her mentor and friend Tessa Strickland. Kate also writes picture books under her pseudonym, Sunny Scribens, and enjoys teaching creative writing to children and adults. She holds an M.A. in Classics from the University of Texas and is also a published poet and scholar. Kate lives with her husband and daughter, and is still a chatterbox with a wild imagination.

David Dean has always loved drawing. Once, when he was very small, a doctor asked him to draw some simple shapes to check his coordination — and he drew a Fiat 127! (That's a kind of car.) Today, David is an award-winning full-time illustrator known for his bright and lively style and dramatic compositions. He has also illustrated *Barefoot Books World Atlas* and the accompanying Barefoot World Atlas App for iPad and iPhone, which was named one of the top ten best apps in the Apple App Store. Today David lives and works in northwest England, and says he still overcomplicates things when asked to draw something simple.